SEASONAL WEATHER

SPRING WEATHER

John Mason

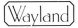

Seasonal Weather

Spring Weather
Summer Weather
Autumn Weather
Winter Weather

Cover: Cherry blossom in a Japanese garden in spring.

Opposite: Dark rain clouds gather in the distance, as a rainbow forms over a
field of ripening corn in spring.

Edited by Sarah Doughty
Series designed by Derek Lee

First published in 1990 by
Wayland (Publishers) Ltd
61, Western Road, Hove
East Sussex, BN3 1JD, England

British Library Cataloguing in Publication Data
Mason, John
  Spring weather
  1. Climate
  I. Title II. Series
  551.6

ISBN 1–85210–941–6

Typeset by Nicola Taylor, Wayland
Printed and bound by Casterman S.A., Belgium

CONTENTS

What is spring?	4
The Earth and the seasons	6
The spring season	8
The Earth's atmosphere	10
The wind	12
Clouds and the water cycle	14
Weather systems and fronts	16
Spring in temperate lands	18
Spring around the world	20
Rainbows and haloes	22
The ozone hole	24
Weather forecasting	26
Things to do – measuring rainfall	28
Glossary	30
Books to read	31
Index	32

What is spring?

In parts of the world there are clear changes in the weather during the year. These changes are called seasons. There are four seasons – spring, summer, autumn and winter. Each season has a particular type of weather, and is marked by differences in the length of day and night. The long days have plenty of sunshine, and it is warmer than when days are short.

In the **tropics** it is always warm. Day and night are of roughly equal length all year.

Close to the **Equator** it is very hot with heavy rain throughout the year. Elsewhere in the tropics there is a hot, wet season and a cooler, dry season. Near the **poles** it is always bitterly cold. There are only two real seasons, summer and winter, but the **Arctic** has a short spring and autumn with warmer temperatures. Only in the mild **temperate regions** which lie between the polar regions and the tropics are changes between all four seasons very marked.

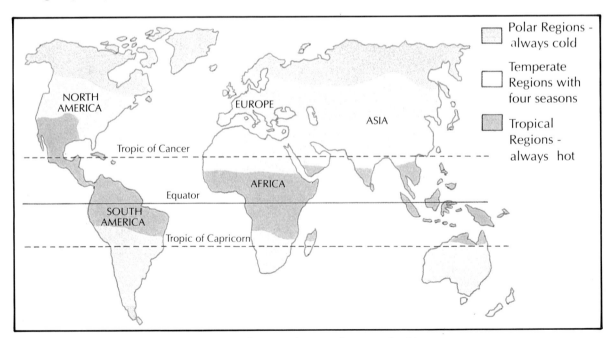

A map of the world showing the main regions of climate.

Colourful alpine flowers carpet the mountain slopes in spring.

Spring occurs as winter changes to summer. Short, cold winter days gradually become longer and warmer. The Sun rises higher in the sky and sets later each evening. As the hours of daylight grow longer and the nights shorter and warmer, we feel the approach of summer.

The Earth and the seasons

Every year the Earth moves round the Sun. The Earth spins on its **axis** which leans over at an angle of 23.5°. This tilt means that as the Earth travels round the Sun, first the northern **hemisphere**, then the southern hemisphere is tilted towards the Sun.

Northern Hemisphere			
Autumn	Winter	Spring	Summer
September	December	March	June
October	January	April	July
November	February	May	August
Spring	Summer	Autumn	Winter
Southern Hemisphere			

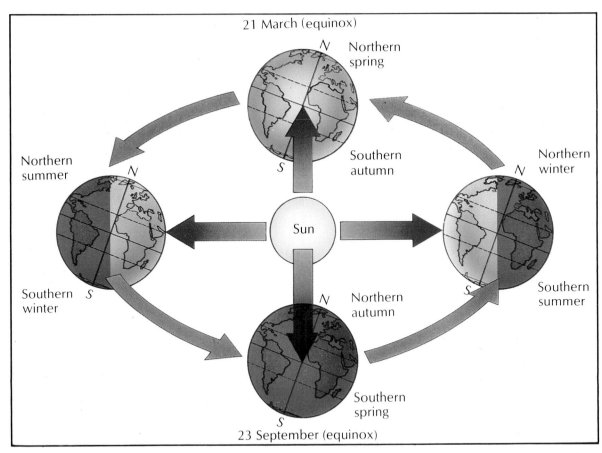

As the Earth travels around the Sun each year, the tilt of its axis affects the amount of sunlight and heat that reaches different parts of the Earth through the year. This gives us the changing seasons.

Each hemisphere in turn receives more sunlight and heat than the other. The amount of heat received at any place varies through the year. This causes the seasons.

Between 21 March and 23 September, the northern hemisphere is tilted towards the Sun. This means that in temperate regions the days are long, the nights are short and the weather is warm. At the same time in the southern hemisphere, the Sun remains lower in the sky, the days are short, and the weather is cold. Between 23 September and 21 March, the reverse is true and it is cold in the northern hemisphere and warm in the south.

As the seasons are reversed in the two hemispheres, when it is spring in one hemisphere it is autumn in the other. The northern spring begins about 21 March. In the southern hemisphere, this is about the start of autumn. Southern spring begins about 23 September, the beginning of the northern autumn. Both these dates mark the time of year when day and night are of equal length all over the world. They are called equinoxes.

It is October and jacaranda trees are blossoming in the Botanical Gardens in Sydney, Australia in spring. At the same time in the northern hemisphere, leaves are falling from the trees and it is autumn.

The spring season

Spring weather can be very unsettled. Many days are warm and sunny, but it can get cold at night. In early spring there can be heavy frosts and fog on cold nights. Spring is cooler than autumn because it takes time for the spring sunshine to melt snow and ice from the cold winter season. Only then can the Sun begin to warm the land, sea and air. With the increasing warmth, plants begin to grow, new crops are planted, and flowers start to bloom in gardens and in the countryside.

Spring occurs early in the temperate regions near the tropics. Here the weather is always warmer. By mid-April, southern California in the USA, and the Mediterranean countries can be as warm as Britain or Belgium in midsummer. In temperate lands near the polar regions, spring arrives later.

As spring sunshine melts snow and ice that have built up during the winter, there may be flooding. In the mountains, sunshine, warm rain and wind may loosen huge masses of snow on

Early spring is a busy time for farmers. When the frost and snow have melted, farmers plough their fields ready for planting crops.

8

◄ Low cloud and mist linger on a rainy spring day over the mountains in County Down, Northern Ireland.

▼ An avalanche crashes down a mountain slope in the French Alps.

mountain slopes. These **avalanches** crash down on valleys below and can be very destructive. In the European Alps, whole villages have been swept away or buried by avalanches.

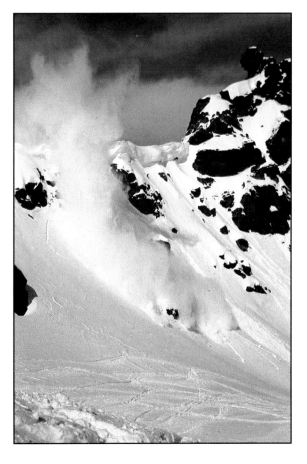

Fastest Avalanches

One of the fastest avalanches occurred at Glarnisch in Switzerland on 6 March 1898.

Snow travelled down a 44° slope at an average speed of 349 km/h covering a distance of 6.9 km in 72 seconds.

The Earth's atmosphere

Seen from space, the Earth is partly hidden by clouds. Clouds occur only in the layer of the **atmosphere** nearest the ground. Nine-tenths of the Earth's air is contained in this shallow layer, called the troposphere. It extends upwards to a height of about 8 km at the poles and 16 km at the Equator.

All the Earth's weather systems occur in the troposphere. It consists mainly of the gases nitrogen and oxygen, with a little carbon dioxide and water vapour. The water vapour produces the clouds which give us rain, hail and snow.

Above the troposphere, the air gets thinner. A layer called the stratosphere reaches a height of about 50 km. It contains a small amount of the gas **ozone**, which as we shall see later is very important. Above the stratosphere lies another layer, the mesosphere. Beyond this, the ionosphere extends into space.

The main zones and temperatures up through the atmosphere.

10

▲ **The Moon rising above the upper layers of the Earth's atmosphere.**

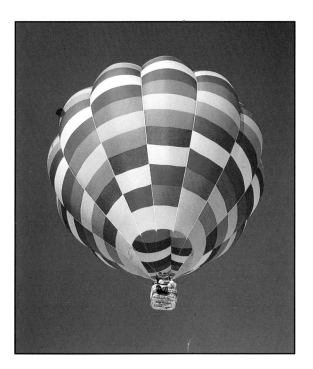

The air in the atmosphere pushes down on the Earth's surface causing **air pressure**. Because the air gets thinner, air pressure gets less as one travels upwards. Air pressure also varies from one place to another on the Earth's surface. Differences in air pressure in different parts of the world creates the Earth's winds.

◀ **As the hot-air balloon rises the air pressure around it lessens.**

The wind

The Earth's winds are created by differences in air pressure. The Sun heats the Earth unevenly, causing air in some places to be warmer than air in other parts. Warm air expands and becomes lighter. It rises creating an area of low pressure beneath it. Cool air is heavier and it sinks, forming a region of high pressure. Air will always try to move from high pressure towards low pressure, causing winds to blow.

Strong winds that usually blow from the same direction are called prevailing winds. Trade Winds, Westerlies and Polar Easterlies are the Earth's main prevailing winds. However, sometimes there are variations in the wind patterns. These occur near oceans and lakes or within local regions of high or low pressure air. This may cause local winds to blow.

Strong local winds often blow in spring. Cold, northerly mistral winds are common in southern France, and they become stronger as they blow down the Rhône valley.

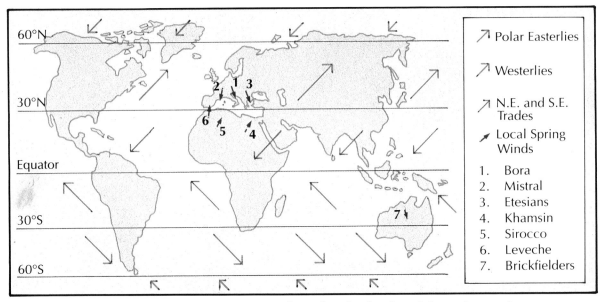

The world's major winds and some local winds that blow in spring.

Similar winds occur in the northern Adriatic (the bora) and Aegean Seas (the etesians) when cold northerly winds are forced up over the mountains.

Warm, dry southerly winds blow across North Africa in late spring, becoming moist if they travel over the sea. These are called the sirocco in Algeria, the leveche in south-east Spain and the khamsin in Egypt and the eastern Mediterranean. Hot, dry northerly winds named brickfielders blow over central Australia.

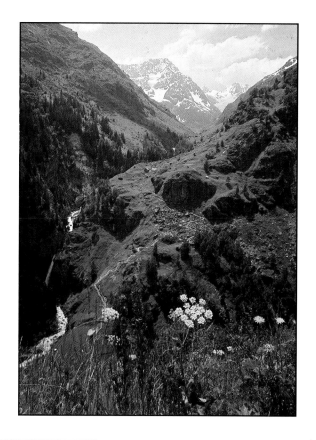

▲ A strong northerly wind, the mistral, sometimes blows down the beautiful Rhône Valley, France, in spring.

◀ A tree on Norfolk Island, lying east of Australia that has been bent by the prevailing wind.

Clouds and the water cycle

As the Sun warms the oceans, some water **evaporates** and turns into water vapour. Wherever air is warmed over sea or land, it absorbs water vapour, because warm air can hold more water vapour than cold air. As the warm air rises it cools, and becomes less able to hold so much water vapour. At the **dewpoint** temperature, some of the water vapour **condenses** into small water droplets. These collect together to become visible as clouds.

If a cloud is blown into a patch of warmer air, some of the droplets turn back into water vapour and the cloud gets smaller. If the cloud is cooled, more water vapour condenses and the cloud grows. Cooled further still, the water droplets grow so large that they fall to the ground as rain, hail or snow.

Over land, rain sinks into the soil and is taken in by plants. Some of this moisture is given off by the plants' leaves and returned to the air.

Dark rain clouds bring showers during unsettled days in spring.

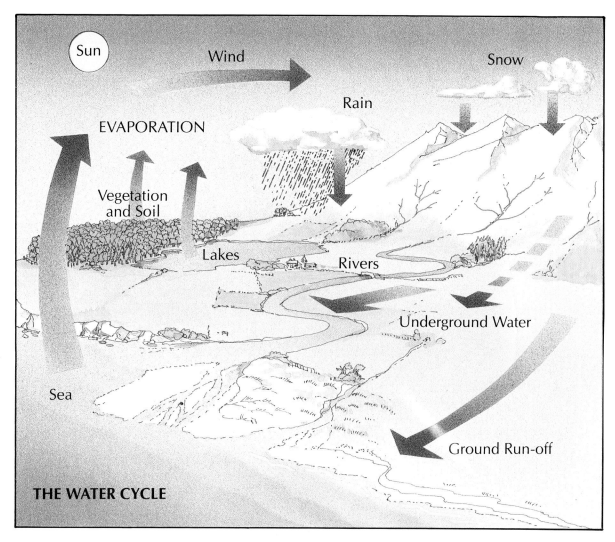

Sun

Wind

Snow

Rain

EVAPORATION

Vegetation and Soil

Lakes

Rivers

Underground Water

Sea

Ground Run-off

THE WATER CYCLE

The sea loses water through evaporation to form clouds. The precipitation from clouds often falls over land and runs back down to the sea.

Some water sinks deep into the soil and rocks below. Some rocks allow this ground water to seep through. It returns to the surface as springs, the sources of rivers.

Surface water flows directly into rivers and streams. All the water eventually reaches the sea and the process is repeated. This continual movement of water is called the water cycle.

Weather systems and fronts

An area of high pressure air is called an anticyclone. In an anticyclone, cool air is slowly sinking. As it does so, it warms and dries out. In late spring, high pressure usually brings warm, dry weather. In a low-pressure region or depression, warm air is rising, cooling and becoming wetter. This leads to the formation of clouds and rain. Depressions usually bring wet or stormy weather. As the winds blow, they cause the regions of high pressure and low pressure to move.

Cold and warm air do not mix. When they meet along a line called a **front**, the heavier cool air forces itself under the warm air, pushing it upwards. Clouds form along the front,

ANTICYCLONE

Cold Air

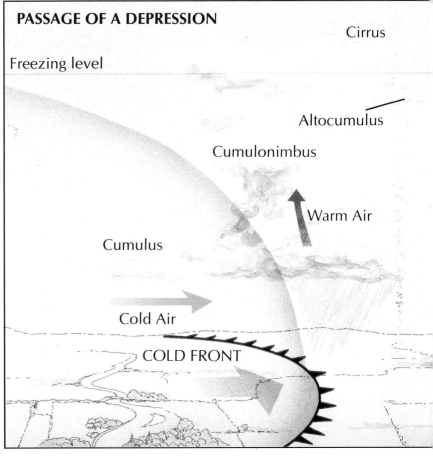

PASSAGE OF A DEPRESSION

Cirrus

Freezing level

Altocumulus

Cumulonimbus

Warm Air

Cumulus

Cold Air

COLD FRONT

bringing rain. Fronts may travel quite fast and rain showers can be quickly followed by bright sunshine. Such changeable weather is common in spring over northern Europe, where fronts sweep in overland from the Atlantic Ocean.

More settled weather occurs in other parts of the world, particularly near the tropics. In the centre of large continental land masses in late spring, the Sun's heat causes the air above the ground to rise and depressions form. Some of these regions have heavy rain in the late afternoon as warm, moist air rises and cools forming clouds that may bring heavy showers.

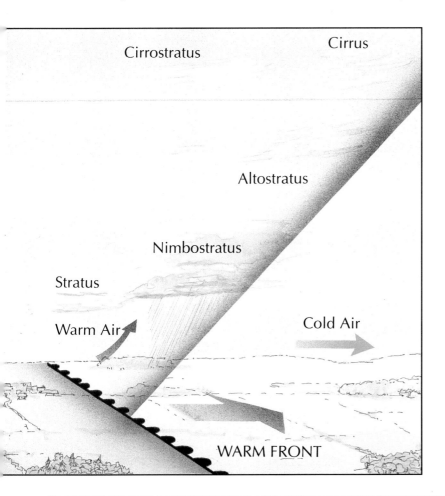

(Far left) In an anticyclone, cold air is sinking. As it does so it warms and dries out.

(Left) Two fronts are formed around a depression; a warm front ahead and a cold front behind. At the warm front, the warm air rises over cold air, condenses and heavy clouds and rain form. At a cold front, the heavier cold air wedges under warm air ahead of it. As the warm air is pushed upwards, clouds and rain occur.

Spring in temperate lands

In northern Europe, the weather is quite changeable from early April until June. However, spring is the driest season of the year in the British Isles, northern France, northern Germany and Scandinavia, although it can be cool and cloudy. Cool temperatures are usual in early May, but later in May and early June, warm, dry rather settled weather is more common.

In Mediterranean countries, the long, unsettled spring lasts from March to May, with

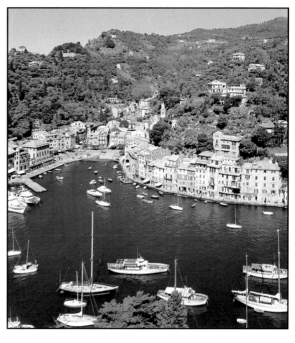

▲ **A fine spring day in the Mediterranean harbour town of Liguria, in Italy.**

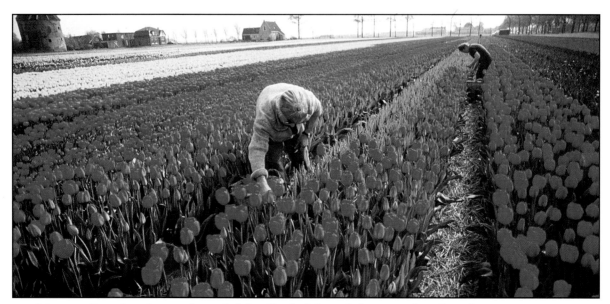

Picking tulips in the colourful bulb fields of the Netherlands.

many false starts of summer weather. April is usually a dry month in the eastern Mediterranean. Cyprus normally has only three days with 1 mm of rainfall or more, but can get heavy rain when depressions move north-eastwards from north Africa. In March 1966, a depression moving across the eastern Mediterranean brought 70 mm of rain to the Hanegev Desert in Israel in just four hours.

Near the polar regions, spring comes late. In northern parts of Canada and the USSR, snow may not start to thaw until late May, but most has gone by late June or early July. By late July, sea ice near the Arctic is breaking up. Snowstorms and heavy frosts may occur as late as mid-June.

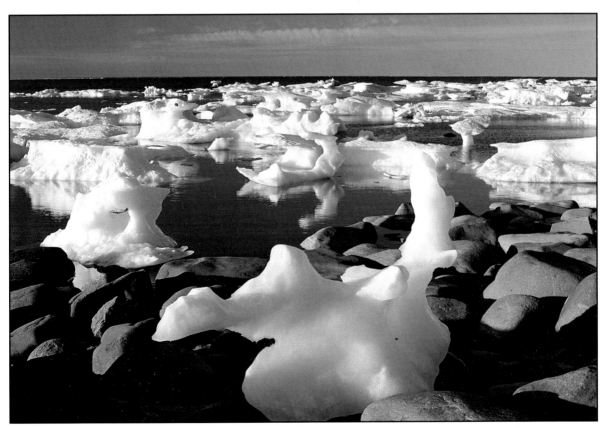

Sea ice breaking up in the spring sunshine in Hudson Bay, Canada.

Spring around the world

In some parts of the world, the change from winter to summer is sudden, with hardly any spring in between. This occurs in the centre of large continental land masses. In only a week or two, snow on the ground melts and temperatures soar towards summer levels. In the Mississippi Valley and the great plains of North America, warm southerly winds sweep up from the Gulf of Mexico. They not only melt the snow, but create fierce whirlwinds called tornadoes which hurl trees and houses into the air and overturn cars.

Between March and May in southern Asia, the Sun moves northwards, heating the land and the air above it. This warm air rises, creating a marked area of low pressure. In early June, south-east Trade

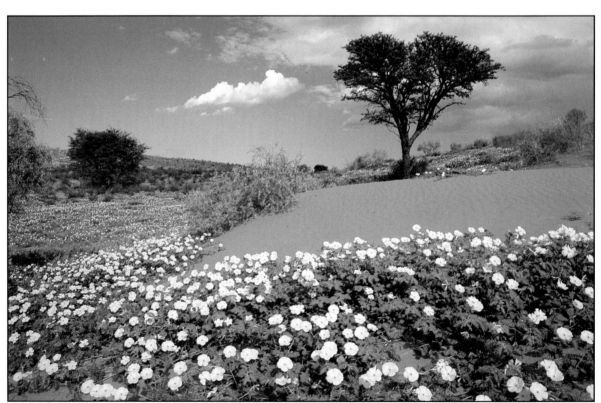

Flowers growing in the Kalahari Desert, Africa after heavy rain.

Winds are sucked across the Equator into this low-pressure region, becoming south-west winds. These **monsoon** winds are warm and moist, and when they reach land, they produce heavy rain.

In the dry desert regions of the world, spring-like weather happens only when there is a very rare fall of rain. It is not a true season, but flowers and other plants suddenly appear immediately after the first rains, as though it were the spring season.

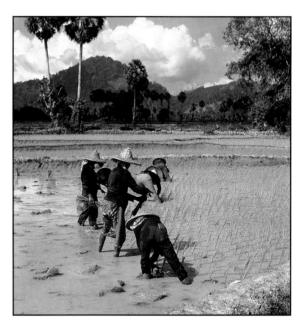

▲ **Planting rice seedlings in the paddy fields of southern Thailand before the monsoon rains arrive.**

Spring Tornadoes

In the spring of 1977 violent tornadoes occurred in the Madaripur district of Bangladesh, about 130 km from Dacca.

Over 500 people were killed, more than 6,000 injured and hundreds of thousands made homeless.

The dark funnel of a spring tornado touches down 50 km east of Phoenix, Arizona, USA.

Rainbows and haloes

A rainbow may be seen if the Sun is fairly low in the sky and breaks through the clouds, shining brightly, while rain is falling. A raindrop can 'break up' sunlight into the colours of the **spectrum**, just like a glass prism does. You have to stand with the Sun behind you, and be looking towards the falling raindrops to be able to see a rainbow clearly.

Different colours of light are bent or refracted by different amounts as they pass through raindrops. They are reflected off the back of the drops at different angles. If one reflection occurs inside each drop, a primary rainbow forms. This has the strongest colours. The outer edge of the bow is red and the inner edge is violet.

Sun's rays

Secondary bow

Primary bow

When light is refracted through a raindrop and reflected off the back of it, a primary rainbow forms. A secondary rainbow is caused by two reflections in the raindrop.

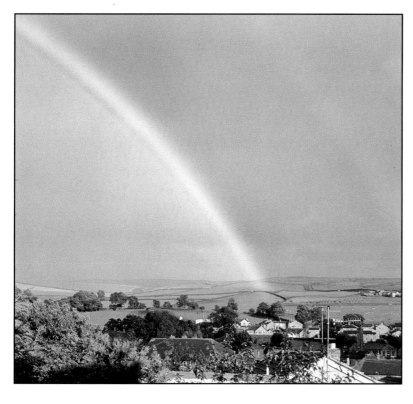

◀ **A primary rainbow, with a fainter, secondary rainbow above it set against dark shower clouds in spring.**

▼ **Mock suns, or sun-dogs, are images of the Sun formed by the refraction of light through ice crystals.**

A secondary rainbow, caused by two reflections, sometimes appears above the primary bow. Its colours are reversed, the outer edge being violet and the inner one red. Its colours are fainter because light is lost at every reflection.

When the Moon shines through thin cloud, it may be surrounded by coloured rings. This is called a corona. Water droplets split the light into coloured bands. If the Sun or

Moon shines through a thin layer of ice crystals, such as **cirrostratus** cloud, a faint coloured halo may be seen around it.

The ozone hole

Sunlight contains more than just the light we can see. Invisible **ultraviolet** rays give sunbathers their summer tan, but over-exposure can cause skin cancer and eye cataracts. Too much ultraviolet also damages plants and life in the sea. Fortunately a thin layer in the stratosphere prevents 90 per cent of the harmful ultraviolet rays from reaching the ground. This is the ozone layer. It lies between 20 km and 35 km above the ground.

A hole in the ozone layer over **Antarctica** was first noticed in October 1982. Nearly all the ozone there is destroyed in the first few weeks of spring. The cause appears to be artificially-made chemicals called **CFCs**. These are used in aerosol cans, fast-food packaging, air-conditioning and refrigerators.

In the darkness of the Antarctic winter, the air is very cold and no wind blows. In these conditions the CFCs

A satellite image of the ozone hole over the South Pole. The hole is the white area with the central black region.

The Ozone Hole

A group of scientific experts found that between 1969 and 1986 there were decreases in ozone of between 1.7 and 3 per cent over Europe, the USA and Japan and much of the USSR, China and the Middle East.

Sunbathers lying out on this beach in Australia are at risk from over-exposure to dangerous ultraviolet rays.

build up. The return of the Sun encourages the CFCs to attack the ozone layer. Later, the wind returns to mix the air. The ozone hole 'repairs' itself, but it never disappears completely.

In October 1987, and again in 1989, the Antarctic ozone hole covered an area the size of the USA. The outcome will be very serious if swift action is not taken to protect the Earth's ozone layer.

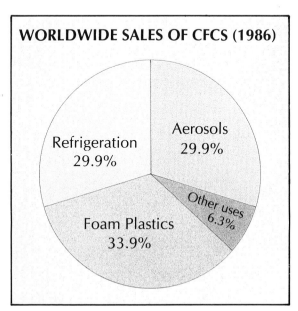

WORLDWIDE SALES OF CFCS (1986)

Refrigeration 29.9%

Aerosols 29.9%

Foam Plastics 33.9%

Other uses 6.3%

CFCs are used all over the world in a variety of products.

Weather forecasting

Information on the weather is collected from weather satellites, balloons, ships, aircraft and local weather stations around the world, and fed into large computers. These calculate the weather conditions at thousands of places on the Earth. The results are drawn on maps to help forecast the weather in the days ahead.

Weather maps show the roughly circular pressure areas, marked 'high' for anticyclones and 'low' for depressions. The lines around the pressure centres are called **isobars**. Winds tend to blow along the isobars. The closer together the isobars, the stronger the winds will blow.

Depressions cause unsettled weather in spring in the temperate regions. Anticyclones usually bring settled weather. In late spring, they may bring a period of warm, sunny days, but earlier in the season they can bring cooler weather and fog.

Fronts are shown on weather maps as lines with triangles (cold fronts), or semicircles (warm fronts) drawn on them. An occluded front occurs when a warm front, which is slow-moving, is overtaken by a faster-moving cold front.

The weather map (opposite) shows a high over parts of the USA in spring. A high over this Texas prairie is causing very fine spring weather.

An occluded front is drawn on a weather map as a line with triangles on one side and semicircles on the other.

Warm fronts move slower than cold fronts because their cool air is heavier and more difficult for the wind to push.

A weather map for a typical April spring day in the USA, showing high and low pressure centres and several fronts.

Things to do – measuring rainfall

To measure the amount of rainfall, you must make a rain gauge.

You will need:

- **A straight-sided glass jar, with a flat bottom, 125 mm in diameter.**
- **A funnel with a top 125 mm across, that will fit into the neck of the glass jar.**
- **A strip of white paper cut to the height of the jar, marked in millimetres by using a ruler.**
- **Waterproof sticky tape.**
- **Modelling clay.**

Stick the paper scale on the outside of the jar using the waterproof tape. Make sure that the scale faces inwards so you can read it by looking through the glass. Check to see that the bottom of the scale is exactly level with the bottom of the jar, allowing for the thickness of the glass.

Place the funnel in the top of the jar. Make sure it is fixed firmly, and that it is watertight by putting a layer of modelling clay between the jar and the funnel.

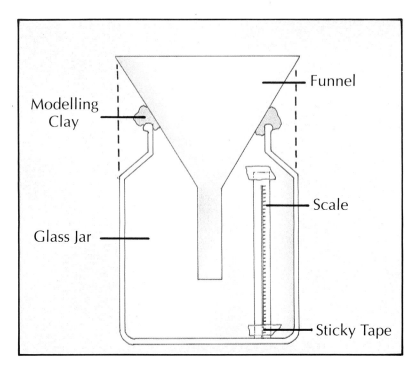

Modelling Clay

Funnel

Scale

Glass Jar

Sticky Tape

A diagram showing how the rain gauge is assembled and made ready for use.

Rainfall measurements:

Day	1	2	3	4	5	6	7	8	9	10	11	12	13	14	15
mm	1·6	9·4	0	1·6	0	4·2	0	0·1	1·2	2·8	0	2·0	0	15	4·1

16	17	18	19	20	21	22	23	24	25	26	27	28	29	30	31
										9·3	2·7	0·6	0·2	0·5	0

Above is a table of rainfall measurements for a month in spring. The results can be displayed as a graph, such as the bar chart shown here.

Position your rain gauge outside on an open area of ground away from buildings and trees. Record the depth of rainwater in it each day at the same time, then empty it and dry it carefully.

By recording your daily measurements in a notebook, you can total up the rainfall for each month. At the end of the year, you can draw a graph of weekly or monthly rainfall totals.

GLOSSARY

Air pressure A force exerted by layers of air on those below and on the ground.

Antarctica The very cold land mass at the South Pole.

Arctic The cold lands and seas around the North Pole.

Atmosphere The thin layer of gases surrounding the Earth.

Avalanche A mass of snow and ice that slides rapidly down the slopes of a mountain.

Axis An imaginary line about which the Earth spins once every day.

CFCs Artificially-made chemicals called chlorofluorocarbons that can damage the ozone layer.

Cirrostratus Thin milky-coloured cloud that often produces rain.

Condense When water vapour turns into drops of liquid by cooling.

Dewpoint The temperature at which water vapour turns into drops of liquid by cooling.

Equator An imaginary line encircling the Earth midway between the North and South Poles.

Evaporate When liquid water becomes a vapour or gas due to heating.

Front The boundary between regions of warm and cooler air.

Hemisphere Half of the globe, divided into north and south.

Isobar A line on a weather map joining places with the same air pressure.

Monsoon A wind that changes direction with the seasons.

Ozone A gas found in the stratosphere which filters out harmful ultraviolet rays from sunlight.

Poles The extreme north and south points on the Earth.

Spectrum The colours produced (red, orange, yellow, green, blue, indigo, violet) when white sunlight is split into its component colours.

Temperate regions The areas between the tropics and the poles that have a moderate, mild climate.

Tropics The areas each side of the Equator that are always warm.

Ultraviolet Invisible rays of light beyond violet in the visible spectrum.

BOOKS TO READ

Lambert, David, **Spring** (Wayland, 1986)
Lambert, David, and Hardy, Ralph, **Weather and its Work** (Orbis, 1985)
McInnes, Celia, **Projects for Spring** (Wayland, 1988)
Rosen, Mike, **Spring Festivals** (Wayland, 1990)
Schopfer, S., **The Young Specialist Looks at Weather** (Burke Publications, 1981)

PICTURE ACKNOWLEDGEMENTS

The publishers would like to thank the following for allowing their photographs to be reproduced in this book: Bruce Coleman Ltd 5 (Hans Reinhard), 19 (Bob and Clara Calhoun), 21 (top) (C.B Frith), 26 (John Shaw); Eye Ubiquitous cover; J.Allen Cash Ltd 9 (top), 13 (both), 14; Oxford Scientific Films 20, 23 (bottom); Photri 11 (top); Science Photo Library 24; Tony Stone Worldwide inside cover, 7, 8, 9 (bottom), 18 (both), 23 (top), 25; Topham 21 (bottom); Zefa 11 (bottom). All illustrations by Malcolm S. Walker except for page 6 by the Hayward Art Group.

INDEX

Numbers in **bold** refer to illustrations

air pressure 11, **11**, 12, 16, 20, 21
Antarctica 24, 25
anticyclone 16, **16–17**, 26
Arctic 4, 19
atmosphere 10, **10**, 11
Australia **7**, 13, **25**
autumn 4, 7, 8
avalanches 9, **9**

Canada 19, **19**
CFCs 24–5, **25**
clouds 10, 14, **14**, 16, 17, 23
corona 23
crops 8, **8**

depression 16, **16–17**, 17, 19, 26
desert 19, **20**, 21

Equator 4, 10
equinox **6**, 7

flooding 8
fog 8, 26
France 18
fronts 16–17, **16–17**, 26–7
frosts 8, 19

hail 10, 14

Italy **18**

Mediterranean 18, **18**, 19
mist **9**

monsoon 21
Moon **11**, 23

Netherlands **18**

ozone 10, 24
  hole **24**, 25

poles 4, 10

rain 4, 10, 14, 16, 17, 19, 21
rainbow 22–3, **22–3**
rainfall
  measuring 28–9, **28–9**

Scandinavia 18
snow 8, 10, 14, 19, 20
summer 4, 5, 19, 20, 24

temperate regions 4, 7, 8, 26
tornadoes 20, **21**
tropics 4, 8, 17

USA 8, 20, **21**, 25, **26**, **27**
USSR 19

water cycle 15, **15**
weather
  information 26
  maps 26–7, **27**
winds 11, 12–13, **12–13**, 16, 20,
  21, 26
winter 4, 5, 8, 20